CLASSIC HAIKU

CLASSIC HAIKU

A Master's Selection

selected and translated by

YUZURU MIURA

CHARLES E. TUTTLE COMPANY
Rutland, Vermont & Tokyo, Japan

Published by the Charles E. Tuttle Company, Inc.
of Rutland, Vermont & Tokyo, Japan
with editorial offices at
2-6 Suido 1-chome, Bunkyo-ku, Tokyo 112

© *1991 by Charles E. Tuttle Publishing Co., Inc.*
All rights reserved

LCC Card No. 91-66031
ISBN 0-8048-1682-4

First edition, 1991
Third printing, 1997

Printed in Singapore

CONTENTS

Note: Japanese name order, surname followed by given name, has been used except on the cover and title page. Macrons in romanized Japanese signify long vowels.

PREFACE

A Japanese haiku is a microcosm composed of seventeen syllables. Within this limited compass, haiku poets are able to express a great variety of feelings and thoughts, at times catching a glimpse of eternity through the evanescent, through the commonplace.

Every great poet, Japanese or otherwise, is a haiku-minded artist, I believe. For example, the mystic poet William Blake, like a traditional haiku poet, could see the world in the palm of a hand, could imagine the cosmos in a small wildflower by the roadside.

On the following pages are English translations of one hundred Japanese haiku written by ancient greats—Bashō, Buson, and Issa—and celebrated moderns—Shiki, Kyoshi, and Dakotsu. As the criterion for choosing the poems was literary merit rather than historical significance, Bashō's well-known haiku about the frog and the old pond is not included in the collection. The poet Takahama Kyoshi has stated that Bashō's poem reveals the starting point of Bashō's direct natural description but the poem itself is trite. Written in 1686 when Bashō was 43, the poem is more important for its historical significance than for its artistic attainment.

For people unfamiliar with Chinese characters, each haiku in the volume is printed in romaji, the romanized form of Japanese. An additional reason for including the romaji is that although the assonance, onomatopoeia, and other poetic features of the original Japanese cannot be satisfactorily reproduced in English translation, such features are apparent in the romaji.

The Japanese original appears in three lines without punctuation; the romaji is rendered in three lines, often of five, seven, and five syllables; the English translation also uses three lines. Of course, literal translation of Japanese to English is difficult—too often unnatural and distorted—and lines in English translation cannot always correspond to lines written in romaji. Above all, my chief intent in presenting these translations has been to convey the poetic essence of the originals.

Haiku are inseparable from the changing seasons, and the one hundred poems of this book fall into haiku's five traditional categories: spring, summer, fall, winter, and New Year's. The number of poems within each category differs because artistic worth is more important than numerical arrangement.

One way to think of a haiku is as a kind of word picture dotted with images on its canvas. Such thinking led to the inclusion of illustrations and calligraphy to accompany certain poems.

Composing verse in the traditional seventeen-syllable form remains very popular in modern Japan. I sincerely hope that this little book will be a great help in promoting haiku in both the East and the West.

For the publication of this book I am grateful to the staff of the Charles E. Tuttle Company; to Mrs. Katō Kōko, president of the *Kō* Poetry Association, member of the managing board of the Museum of Haiku Literature, and councilor of the International Haiku Association; to Mr. Ishizaki Ryokufū, a leading staff member of the haiku magazine *Kō;* and to the internationally famous painter Saitō Gorō and the calligrapher Yokoi Enshū, who amused our eyes with beautiful illustrations and dynamic calligraphy. I take this opportunity to thank again these persons.

—Miura Yuzuru

Nagoya, Japan

CLASSIC HAIKU

SPRING

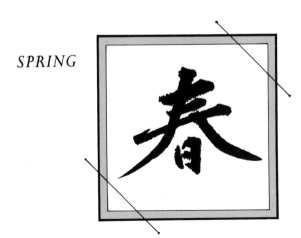

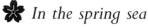 *In the spring sea*
   Waves undulating and undulating
   All day long.

Haru no umi
   Hinemosu
      Notari notari kana

—YOSA BUSON

Yosa Buson (1716–84) was a leading poet of the late eighteenth century and also a distinguished painter. His poetry is pictorial, romantically lyrical, and often displays a delicate sensitivity.

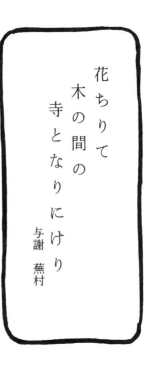

With the cherry blossoms gone
The temple is glimpsed
Through twigs and branches.

Hana chirite
Ko-no-ma no
Tera to nari ni keri

—YOSA BUSON

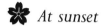 *At sunset*
   The sound of pheasant shooting
      Near the spring mountainside.

Hi kururu ni
   Kiji utsu
      Haru no yama-be kana

—YOSA BUSON

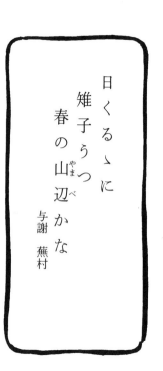

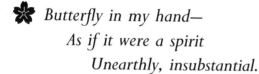 *Butterfly in my hand—*
As if it were a spirit
Unearthly, insubstantial.

Utsutsu naki
Tsumami-gokoro no
Kochō kana

—YOSA BUSON

うつゝなき
つまみごゝろの
胡蝶哉

与謝　蕪村

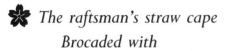 *The raftsman's straw cape*
 Brocaded with
  The storm-strewn cherry blossoms.

Ikada-shi no
 Mino ya arashi no
  Hana-goromo

—YOSA BUSON

筏
士
の

蓑
や
あ
ら
し
の

花
衣

与
謝　
蕪
村

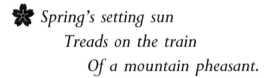 *Spring's setting sun*
    Treads on the train
        Of a mountain pheasant.

Yama-dori no
    O o fumu haru no
        Iri-hi kana

—YOSA BUSON

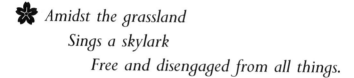 *Amidst the grassland*
Sings a skylark
Free and disengaged from all things.

Hara-naka ya
Mono nimo tsukazu
Naku hibari

—MATSUO BASHŌ

原中や
物にもつかず
鳴雲雀

松尾　芭蕉

Matsuo Bashō (1644–94) elevated haiku to the art form. One critic has called Bashō a Wordsworthian figure who sought a mystical union with nature. With interest in haiku spreading throughout the world, Bashō's name has become internationally known.

A fallen camellia
On a rock
In the rapids.

Kyūtan no
Iwao no ue no
Ochi tsubaki

—MIURA YUZURU

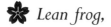 *Lean frog,*
   Don't be defeated!
      Issa is here cheering you.

Yase-gaeru

   Makeru na Issa

      Kore ni ari

—KOBAYASHI ISSA

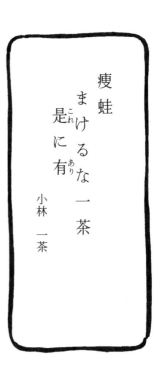

Kobayashi Issa (1763–1827) was born in Shinano (now Niigata prefecture) the first son of a farmer. His mother died when he was three, and five years later his father remarried. The stepmother was cold to Issa, and Issa struggled with family troubles all his life. At the age of fourteen he left Shinano for Edo (Tokyo) and began to study haiku. His haiku are characterized by down-to-earth expressions and animal images.

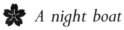 *A night boat*
    Sails away
        Illuminated by a wildfire.

Yama-yake no
    Akari ni kudaru
        Yobune kana

               —KOBAYASHI ISSA

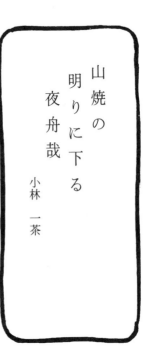

山焼の
明りに下る
夜舟哉

小林　一茶

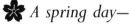 *A spring day—*
  A long line of footprints
   On the sandy beach.

Suna-hama ni
  Ashi-ato nagaki
   Haru hi kana

    —MASAOKA SHIKI

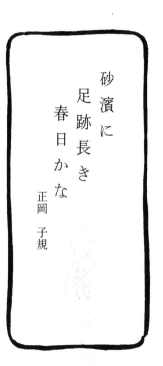

In his youth Masaoka Shiki (1867–1902) contracted tuberculosis and became an invalid. He devoted his life to literature, writing essays, haiku, and tanka (traditional thirty-one syllable poems). Shiki pushed forward a major reform of haiku by advocating the writing of *shasei* (sketches from life). In 1897 he initiated the haiku magazine *Hototogisu* (cuckoo).

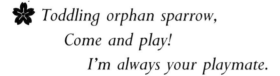 *Toddling orphan sparrow,*
Come and play!
I'm always your playmate.

Ware to kite
Asobe ya oya no
Nai suzume

—KOBAYASHI ISSA

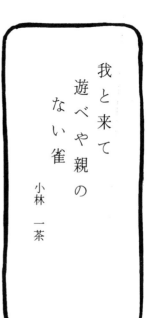

我と来て
遊べや親の
ない雀

小林　一茶

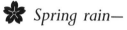 *Spring rain—*
    A thrown-away letter
      Windblown in the grove.

Haru-same ya
    Yabu ni fukaruru
      Sute tegami

          —KOBAYASHI ISSA

春雨や
藪に吹かるゝ
捨手紙

小林　一茶

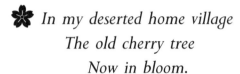 *In my deserted home village*
The old cherry tree
Now in bloom.

Mikagirishi
   Kokyō no sakura
     Saki ni keri

—KOBAYASHI ISSA

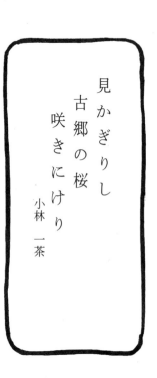

見かぎりし
古郷の桜
咲きにけり
小林　一茶

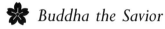 *Buddha the Savior*
Gets offerings of flowers and money
Even while sleeping.

Mi-hotoke ya
　　Nete gozattemo
　　　　Hana to zeni

　　　　　　　—KOBAYASHI ISSA

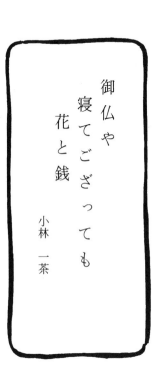

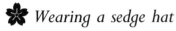 *Wearing a sedge hat*
A maiden looks in the mirror
Oblivious of picking tea leaves.

Suge-gasa o
    Kite kagami miru
        Chatsumi kana

—KAGAMI SHIKŌ

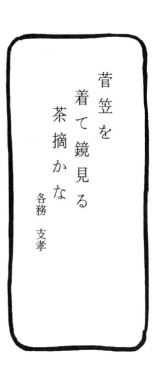

Kagami Shikō (1665–1731) was one of the ten major disciples of Bashō. He wrote the first critical essay on Bashō and is credited with popularizing Bashō's work throughout the country.

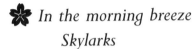 *In the morning breeze*
  Skylarks
    Dance straight up in the sky.

Asa-kaze ya
  Tada hito-suji ni
    Age-hibari

—ŌSHIMA RYŌTA

Ōshima Ryōta (1718–87) avoided the witty, urbane style of haiku prevalent in the mid-eighteenth century and prompted a return of the original principles of Bashō. He was an excellent teacher and had two thousand pupils at one time.

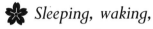 *Sleeping, waking,*
   And then giving a great yawn,
     The cat goes out for lovemaking.

Nete okite
  Ō-akubi shite
    Neko no koi

      —KOBAYASHI ISSA

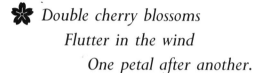 *Double cherry blossoms*
   Flutter in the wind
      One petal after another.

Hito-e zutsu
   Hito-e zutsu chire
      Yae-zakura

—MASAOKA SHIKI

Note: Double-petaled cherry blossoms are deeper in color than single ones and have a later blooming season.

 *Woodcarved dolls—*
August countenances
From bygone days.

Tōtsu-yo no
Omowa kashikoshi
Kibori-bina

—MIZUHARA SHŪOSHI

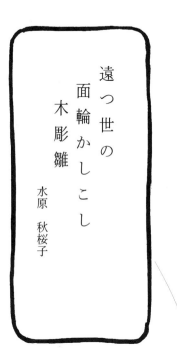

遠つ世の
面輪かしこし
木彫雛

水原　秋桜子

Mizuhara Shūōshi (1892–1981), born in Tokyo the eldest son of a physician, started practicing medicine at his father's clinic in 1928. As an undergraduate at Tokyo University he had first written tanka and later haiku. His first volume of haiku, *Katsushika,* was published in 1930.

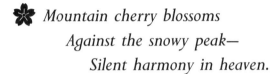 *Mountain cherry blossoms*
Against the snowy peak—
Silent harmony in heaven.

Yama-zakura
　Setsu-rei ten ni
　　Koe mo nashi

　　　　　—MIZUHARA SHŪŌSHI

山桜
雪嶺天に
声もなし

水原　秋桜子

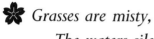 *Grasses are misty,*
The waters silent—
A tranquil evening.

Kusa kasumi
Mizu ni koe naki
Hi-gure kana

—YOSA BUSON

草霞み
水に聲なき
日暮かな

与謝　蕪村

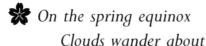 *On the spring equinox*
Clouds wander about
The entrance of a mountain temple.

Yama-dera no
　To ni kumo asobu
　　Higan kana

—IIDA DAKOTSU

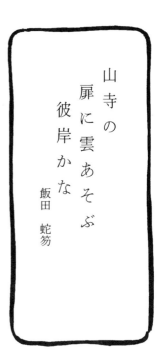

山寺の
扉に雲あそぶ
彼岸かな
　　飯田　蛇笏

Iida Dakotsu (1885–1962) was born in a village near Mt. Fuji. He studied English literature at Waseda University but in 1909 left Waseda and returned home. In that quiet environment he devoted himself to haiku, turning the local magazine *Ummo* (isinglass) into one of the finest publications of its kind. His haiku are characterized by a dynamic description of nature.

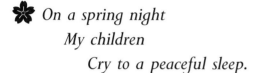 *On a spring night*
   My children
      Cry to a peaceful sleep.

Haru no yo ya
  Naki-nagara neru
    Kodomo-tachi

—MURAKAMI KIJŌ

Murakami Kijō (1865–1930) was born in Tokyo. As a youth he wanted to enter civil service but worsening deafness in his late teens forced him to give up the plan. Throughout his miserable life, writing haiku provided Kijō his only consolation. Under the influence of Takahama Kyoshi, he became one of the major poets of the Hototogisu school of haiku.

Withered lotus leaves,
Some broken, some not,
Float on the spring water.

Kare-hasu no
Oruru wa orete
Haru no mizu

—NAKAMURA TEIJO

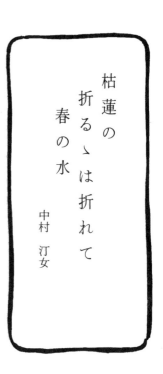

Nakamura Teijo (1900–88) was born in Kumamoto in Kyushu. Her sensitive, feminine haiku are often contrasted with the passionate, masculine haiku of Sugita Hisajo, another leading woman haiku poet. Teijo composed the so-called "kitchen haiku," poems reflecting her everyday life.

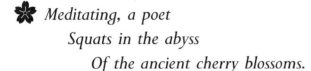 *Meditating, a poet*
   Squats in the abyss
     Of the ancient cherry blossoms.

Inishie no
   Hana no naraku no
     Naka ni zasu

       —KADOKAWA HARUKI

いにしへの
花の奈落の
中に座す

角川　春樹

Born in Tokyo in 1942, Kadokawa Haruki is a publisher, movie producer, and haiku poet. His father, Gen'yoshi, was also a publisher and haiku poet. Collections of Haruki's haiku won the Yomiuri Literary Prize in 1984 and the Dakotsu Award in 1990.

SUMMER

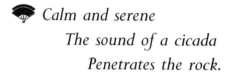 *Calm and serene*
The sound of a cicada
Penetrates the rock.

Shizukasa ya
Iwa ni shimi-iru
Semi no koe

—MATSUO BASHŌ

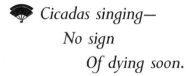 *Cicadas singing—*
  No sign
   Of dying soon.

Yagate shinu
 Keshiki wa miezu
  Semi no koe

   —MATSUO BASHŌ

やがて死ぬ
けしきは見えず
蝉の声

松尾　芭蕉

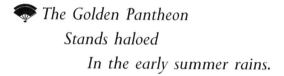 *The Golden Pantheon*
    Stands haloed
       In the early summer rains.

Samidare no
    Furi-nokoshite ya
        Hikari-dō

          —MATSUO BASHŌ

Note: The Golden Pantheon, or Hikari-dō, is part of Chūson-ji, the main temple of the Tendai sect of Buddhism, and is located in Hiraizumi in Iwate prefecture. The ceiling and floor of the Golden Pantheon are covered with gold leaf. It dates from the early twelfth century. The remains of three Fujiwara rulers—Motohira, Hidehira, and Yasuhira—are entombed here.

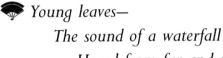 *Young leaves—*
The sound of a waterfall
Heard from far and near.

Ochi-kochi ni
Taki no oto kiku
Wakaba kana

—YOSA BUSON

遠近に
滝の音聞く
若ばかな

与謝　蕪村

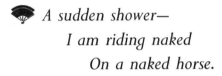 *A sudden shower—*
I am riding naked
On a naked horse.

Yūdachi ya
  Hadaka de norishi
    Hadaka uma

—KOBAYASHI ISSA

夕立や
裸で乗し
はだか馬
　小林　一茶

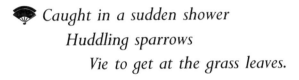 *Caught in a sudden shower*
    Huddling sparrows
        Vie to get at the grass leaves.

Yūdachi ya
    Kusaba o tsukamu
        Mura suzume

          —YOSA BUSON

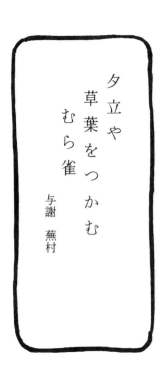

夕立や
草葉をつかむ
むら雀

与謝　蕪村

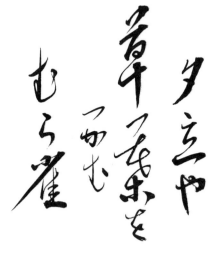

Gargantuan clouds during dog days
   Take the shape of a demon,
      Then change into the Buddha.

Oni to nari
   Hotoke to naru ya
      Doyō-gumo

—KOBAYASHI ISSA

鬼と成り
仏となるや
土用雲

小林 一茶

*The windchime silent
But the clock ticking—
Ah, the heat!*

Fūrin wa
Nara-de tokei no
Atsusa kana

—YOKOI YAYŪ

Yokoi Yayū (1702–83) wrote essays, haiku, and *haibun* (haiku prose). Born in Nagoya the son of a high-ranking official of the Owari domain (now Aichi prefecture), Yayū became a faithful official, but his real interest was literature. After his retirement from official life, he devoted himself to the writing of *haibun* and haiku.

Oh, evening swallow!
    My heart teems with cares and anxieties
        About tomorrow.

Yū tsubame
    Ware niwa asu no
        Ate mo nashi

—KOBAYASHI ISSA

夕
燕

我
に
は
翌_あ
日_す
の

あ
て
も
な
し

小
林

一
茶

The fly
    Wringing its hands and rubbing its feet—
    Don't swat it!

Yare utsu na
  Hae ga te o suri
    Ashi o suru

—KOBAYASHI ISSA

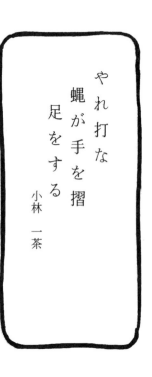

やれ打な
蠅が手を摺
足をする

小林　一茶

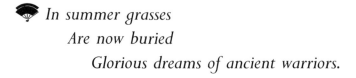 *In summer grasses*
    Are now buried
        Glorious dreams of ancient warriors.

Natsu-kusa ya
    Tsuwa-mono-domo ga
        Yume no ato

—MATSUO BASHŌ

夏草や
兵どもが
ゆめの跡

松尾　芭蕉

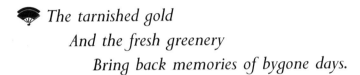 *The tarnished gold*
   And the fresh greenery
      Bring back memories of bygone days.

Kogane sabi
   Wakaba ni shinobu
      Mukashi kana

—MIURA CHORA

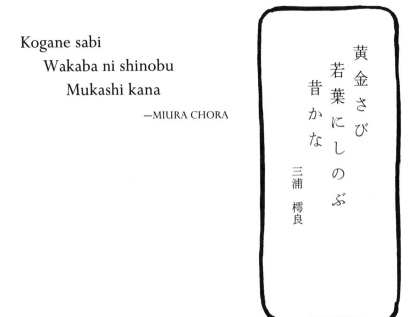

Miura Chora (1729–80), born in Shima province (now part of Mie prefecture), traveled throughout the country composing poems. He was a friend of Yosa Buson and helped lead the haiku revival movement of the eighteenth century.

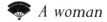 *A woman*
  Taking a bath in a tub
    Is coveted by a crow.

Gyōzui no
  Onna ni horeru
    Karasu kana

—TAKAHAMA KYOSHI

行
水
の
女
に
ほ
れ
る
鳥
か
な

高濱　虚子

Inspired by Shiki, Takahama Kyoshi (1874–1959) was determined to become a man of letters. From about 1913 his interest turned to haiku and he became a prolific poet, writing tens of thousands of poems in the five-seven-five syllable form.

Oppressive heat—
　　My whirling mind
　　　　Listens to the peals of thunder.

Atsukurushi
　　Midare-gokoro ya
　　　　Rai o kiku

—MASAOKA SHIKI

暑くるし
乱れ心や
雷をきく

正岡　子規

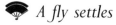 *A fly settles*
　　On the breast
　　　A sleeping babe has forgotten to suck.

Soi-chi-ne no
　Wasure chibusa ni
　　Hae tomaru

—HINO SŌJŌ

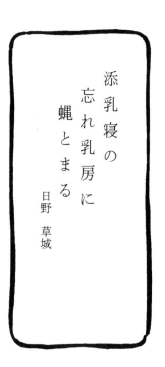

添乳寝の
忘れ乳房に
蠅とまる

日野　草城

After entering the Third National Junior College, Hino Sōjō (1901–56) became the brilliant leader of the student haiku club. In 1935 he initiated the haiku magazine *Kikan* (flagship) and advocated a modern style of haiku. After World War II, his haiku became philosophical.

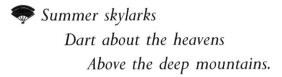

Summer skylarks
Dart about the heavens
Above the deep mountains.

Oku-yama no
Ten o utsurō
Natsu hibari

—IIDA DAKOTSU

奥山の
天をうつろふ
夏雲雀

飯田　蛇笏

A woman dozing—
The breath from her nostrils
Stirs a cool breeze.

Hana no ana
　　Suzushiku nemuru
　　　　Onna kana

　　　　　　　—HINO SŌJŌ

鼻
の
穴

涼
し
く
睡
(ねむ)
る

女
か
な

日
野
　
草
城

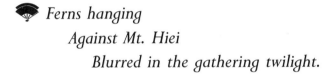 *Ferns hanging*
   Against Mt. Hiei
      Blurred in the gathering twilight.

Iki toshite
   Kururu Hiei to
      Tsuri shinobu

—HINO SŌJŌ

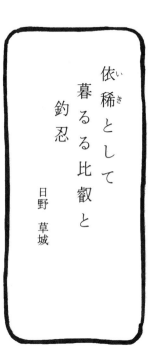

依
稀
と
し
て
暮
る
る
比
叡
と
釣
忍

日野　草城

Note: Mt. Hiei is located on the border between Kyoto and Shiga prefectures in central Japan. On the eastern slope is the temple called Enryaku-ji, a center of the Tendai sect of Buddhism founded in 788.

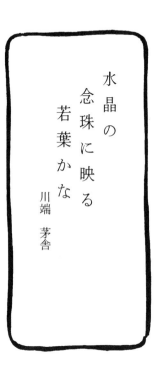

Young green leaves
  Mirrored in the crystal beads
    Of my rosary.

Suishō no
  Nenju ni utsuru
    Wakaba kana

—KAWABATA BŌSHA

Kawabata Bōsha (1900–41) was first interested in painting but then turned to haiku. He was a sickly person, and after he contracted caries of the spine in 1931, writing haiku was his only pastime until he died. The dew was one of his most beloved images. His first volume of haiku contains twenty-six poems on the dew.

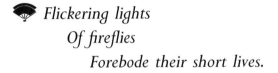 *Flickering lights*
  Of fireflies
    Forebode their short lives.

Meimetsu no
  Izure kanashiki
    Hotaru kana

—KAWABATA BŌSHA

明
滅
の
い
づ
れ
悲
し
き
蛍
か
な

川端　茅舎

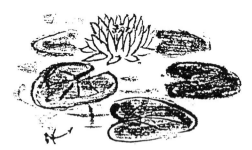

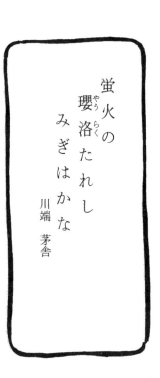

Firefly lights
   Link up as a chain of beads
   Along the water's edge.

Hotaru-bi no
   Yōraku tareshi
   Migiwa kana

—KAWABATA BŌSHA

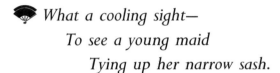 *What a cooling sight—*
To see a young maid
Tying up her narrow sash.

Semaki obi
  Shimete suzushiki
    Tachii kana

      —KUBOTA MANTARŌ

狭き帯
しめて涼しき
立居かな

久保田　万太郎

Kubota Mantarō (1889–1963) was the director of the drama and music department of the Tokyo Broadcasting Station (now NHK). He loved the lifestyle and culture of old downtown Tokyo, and his haiku teem with the pathos and humor of the area's inhabitants.

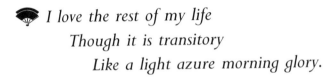 *I love the rest of my life*
Though it is transitory
Like a light azure morning glory.

Asagao no
    Hanada no awaki
        Inochi oshi

—TOMIYASU FŪSEI

Tomiyasu Fūsei (1885–1979) held high administrative posts in government service. In 1928 he became the editor of the haiku section of the literary magazine *Wakaba* (young leaves). In 1937 he retired from civil service and spent most of his time writing haiku.

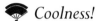 *Coolness!*
  The sound of the bell
    Leaving the bell.

Suzushisa ya
  Kane o hanaruru
    Kane no koe

—YOSA BUSON

涼しさや
鐘を離るゝ
鐘の聲

与謝　蕪村

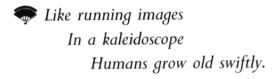 *Like running images*
    In a kaleidoscope
        Humans grow old swiftly.

Sōma-tō
    Nagaruru gotoku
        Hito oyuru

—NISHIJIMA BAKUNAN

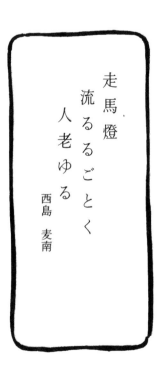

Nishijima Bakunan (1895–1981), a lifetime disciple of Iida Dakotsu, was a humanist of firm character. Right before the end of World War II, he was imprisoned for his antiwar views. He engaged in farming in Kyushu and sought no worldly fame.

A thunderbolt in the rainy season
    Carried away
        My dearest one.

Tsuyu jinrai
   Itoshiki mono o
     Daki yukishi

—NOZAWA SETSUKO

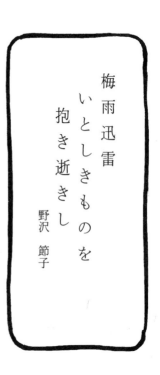

梅雨迅雷
いとしきものを
抱き逝きし
野沢　節子

Note: The poem was written on the death of Miss Takahashi Tsuruko.

Born in Yokohama in 1920, Nozawa Setsuko left school in her teens because of caries and spent the next twenty-four years in bed. She became a staff member of the magazine *Hama* (beach), initiated by Ōno Rinka in 1946. In 1972 she founded the magazine *Ran* (orchid).

AUTUMN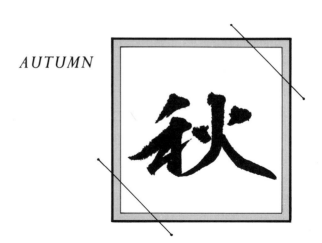

From within the nostrils
Of the colossal Buddha
Comes out this morning's fog.

Daibutsu no
Hana kara detari
Kesa no kiri

—KOBAYASHI ISSA

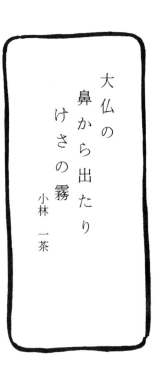

大仏の
鼻から出たり
けさの霧

小林 一茶

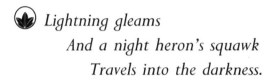 *Lightning gleams*
And a night heron's squawk
Travels into the darkness.

Inazuma ya
Yami no kata yuku
Goi no koe

—MATSUO BASHŌ

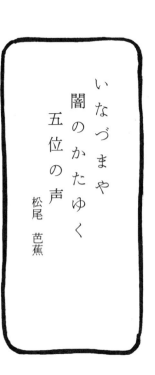

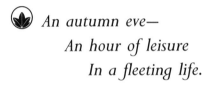 *An autumn eve—*
An hour of leisure
In a fleeting life.

Kagiri aru
  Inochi no hima ya
    Aki no kure

—YOSA BUSON

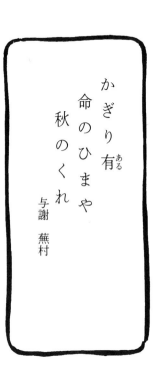

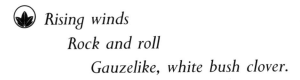 *Rising winds*
  Rock and roll
   Gauzelike, white bush clover.

Kaze tachite
 Hakusa yurugasu
  Midare hagi

    —MIURA YUZURU

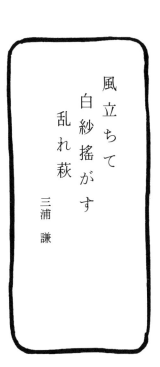

風立ちて
白紗搖がす
乱れ萩

三浦　謙

In the cowshed
  Mosquitoes' faint humming—
    Gusty autumn winds outside.

Ushi-beya ni
  Ka no koe yowashi
    Aki no kaze

—MATSUO BASHŌ

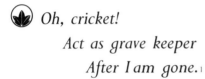 *Oh, cricket!*
   Act as grave keeper
   After I am gone.[1]

Ware shinaba
   Haka-mori to nare
   Kirigirisu

—KOBAYASHI ISSA

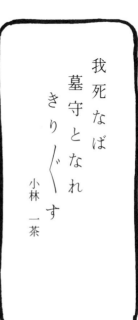

我死なば
墓守となれ
きり〴〵す
小林　一茶

Silent communion
Between the guest,
The host, and the white chrysanthemum.

Mono-iwazu
Kyaku to teishu to
Shira-giku to

—ŌSHIMA RYŌTA

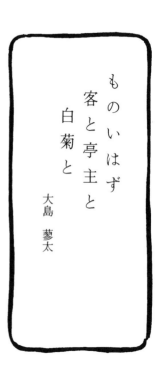

ものいはず
客と亭主と
白菊と

大島 蓼太

Against the bright full moon
A hilltop pine tree
Is the image of my rebirth.

Meigetsu ya
Umare-kawaraba
Mine no matsu

—ŌSHIMA RYŌTA

名月や
生れ変らば
峰の松

大島　蓼太

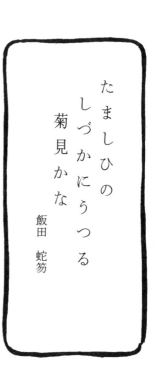

As I view chrysanthemums
   My soul and heart
     Are gently enticed by the floral spirit.

Tamashii no
   Shizuka ni utsuru
     Kikumi kana

          —IIDA DAKOTSU

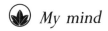 *My mind*
    Is calm and resigned
        As I tread on the fallen leaves.

Ochiba funde
    Hito dōnen o
        Mattō-su

           —IIDA DAKOTSU

落葉ふんで
人道念を
全うす

飯田　蛇笏

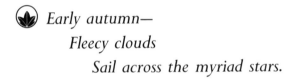 *Early autumn—*
Fleecy clouds
Sail across the myriad stars.

Mura-boshi ni
Usu-gumo wataru
Shoshū kana

—IIDA DAKOTSU

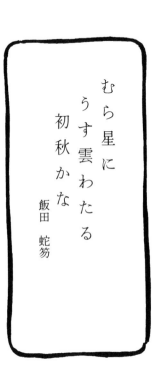

むら星に
うす雲わたる
初秋かな
飯田　蛇笏

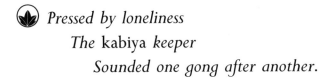 *Pressed by loneliness*
  The kabiya *keeper*
    Sounded one gong after another.

Sabishisa ni
  Mata dora utsu ya
    Kabiya-mori

—HARA SEKITEI

Note: A *kabiya* is a kind of lookout post, from which smoldering wood emits a bad smell to protect crops from foxes and boars. Once a common sight in rural Japan, the *kabiya* has all but disappeared today.

In his youth the favorite theme of Hara Sekitei (1886–1951) was the exuberant nature of Yoshinoyama, the mountains near Yoshino in Nara prefecture. Around 1936 his health declined and his style of haiku changed, as he began writing poems in a light, plain style.

A drop of dew
  Sits on a rock
    Like a diamond.

Kongō no
  Tsuyu hito-tsubu ya
    Ishi no ue

—KAWABATA BŌSHA

金剛の
露ひとつぶや
石の上

川端　茅舎

A woodpecker's drilling
    Echoes
        To the mountain clouds.

Yama-gumo ni
    Kaesu kodama ya
        Kera-tsutsuki

—IIDA DAKOTSU

山雲に
かへす谺(こだま)や
けらつつき

飯田　蛇笏

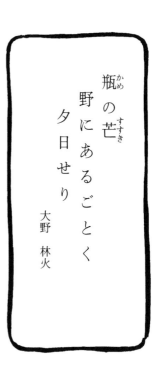

Pampas grass in the vase
  Aglow with the setting sun
    As if in the open field.

Kame no susuki
  No ni aru gotoku
    Yū-hi seri

—ŌNO RINKA

瓶の芒
野にあるごとく
夕日せり

大野　林火

Ōno Rinka (1904–82) graduated from the economics department of Tokyo University. A disciple of the haiku poet Usuda Arō (1879–1951), Rinka initiated the haiku magazine *Hama* (beach) in 1946. His style of haiku remained consistent throughout his life, with a pure lyricism threading his poems.

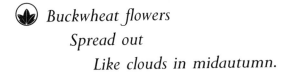 *Buckwheat flowers*
    Spread out
        Like clouds in midautumn.

Chūshū no
    Kumo no gotoku ni
        Soba no hana

—YAMAGUCHI SEISON

Yamaguchi Seison (1892–1989), born in Morioka in Iwate prefecture, loved writing haiku about Michinoku, the northern district of Honshu now comprising Aomori, Iwate, Yamagata, and Fukushima prefectures. He was a professor at Tokyo University and specialized in metallurgy. His haiku reflect the strict eye of a scientist and the innocence of a lover of nature.

Wild, rolling sea—
    The Milky Way
        Hangs over Sado Island.

Ara-umi ya
    Sado ni yokotau
        Ama-no-gawa

—MATSUO BASHŌ

あらうみや
佐渡に横ふ
天の川

松尾　芭蕉

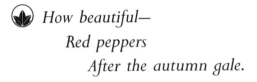 *How beautiful—*
Red peppers
After the autumn gale.

Utsukushi ya
No-waki no ato no
Tōgarashi

—YOSA BUSON

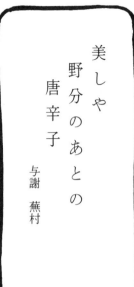

美しや
野分のあとの
唐辛子

与謝　蕪村

The depths of Shiga—
  A field of wildflowers
    Borders the clouds.

Kumo fururu
  Bakari no hana-no
    Shiga no oku

—HOSOMI AYAKO

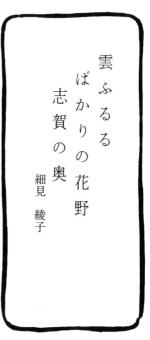

Note: Shiga, a highland in the northeastern part of Nagano prefecture in central Japan, is famous for its dense white-birch forests and alpine flora.

Born in 1907, Hosomi Ayako began her haiku-writing activities around 1930. In 1946 she became a staff member of the haiku magazine *Kaze* (winds), initiated by her husband, Sawaki Kin'ichi. She composes haiku that show a thoughtful, feminine observation.

Red dragonflies
Flowing like a ripple
Toward the crimson sky.

Aka-tombo
Sara-sara nagaru
Akane-zora

—MIURA YUZURU

赤とんぼ
さらさら流る
茜空

三浦　謙

WINTER

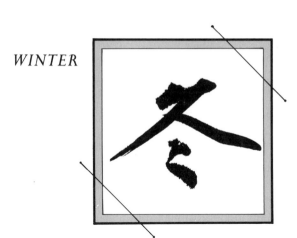

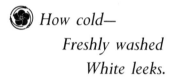 *How cold—*
    Freshly washed
    White leeks.

Negi shiroku
    Araitate taru
        Samusa kana

—MATSUO BASHŌ

葱
白
く
あ
ら
ひ
た
て
た
る
さ
む
さ
哉

松尾　芭蕉

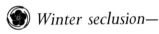 *Winter seclusion—*
The mountains of Yoshino
In my innermost mind.

Fuyu-gomori
  Kokoro no oku no
    Yoshino yama

—YOSA BUSON

Note: The mountains of Yoshino, in Nara prefecture in central Japan, are celebrated for their beautiful cherry blossoms.

 *Sparrows*
   Playing hide-and-seek
      Among the tea blossoms.

Cha no hana ni
   Kakurem-bo suru
      Suzume kana

— KOBAYASHI ISSA

茶
の
花
に
隠
かくれ
ん
ぼ
す
る
雀
哉

小
林
一
茶

When I'm sick on a journey
    Phantoms move about
        Over the desolate moor.

Tabi ni yande
    Yume wa kare-no o
        Kake-meguru

—MATSUO BASHŌ

旅
に
病
で
夢
は
枯
野
を
・
か
け
め
ぐ
る

松尾　芭蕉

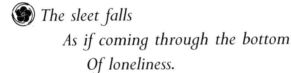 *The sleet falls*
As if coming through the bottom
Of loneliness.

Sabishisa no
　　Soko nukete furu
　　　Mizore kana

—NAITŌ JŌSŌ

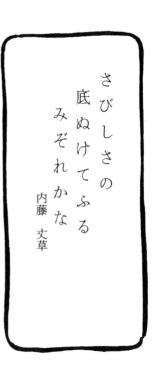

さびしさの
底ぬけてふる
みぞれかな

内藤　丈草

At one time a samurai, Naitō Jōsō (1662–1704) later became a priest and in 1689 joined Bashō's group. Sincere and faithful to his master, he mourned Bashō's death for three years.

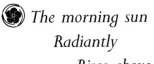 *The morning sun*
    Radiantly
        Rises above the frosty woods.

Ura-ura to
    Asahi izuru shimo no
        Hayashi kana

           —IIDA DAKOTSU

うらうらと
旭いづる霜の
林かな

飯田　蛇笏

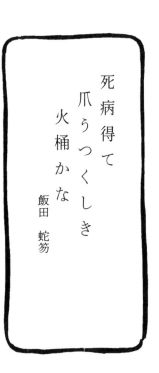

With a fatal disease
   The patient sees
      Her beautiful nails over the brazier.

Shibyō ete
   Tsume utsukushiki
      Hioke kana

—IIDA DAKOTSU

死病得て
爪うつくしき
火桶かな

飯田　蛇笏

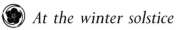 *At the winter solstice*
   The sun permeates the firmament
   Of the mountain province.

Yama-guni no
   Kokū hi wataru
      Tōji kana

—IIDA DAKOTSU

山国の
虚空日わたる
冬至かな

飯田　蛇笏

Under the winter light
  Death is not hesitating
    To destroy the peaceful countenance.

Fuyu-tomoshi
  Shi wa yōgan ni
    Tōkarazu

—IIDA DAKOTSU

冬灯
死は容顔に
遠からず
飯田 蛇笏

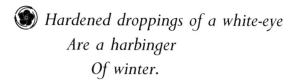 *Hardened droppings of a white-eye*
   Are a harbinger
      Of winter.

Kataku naru
   Mejiro no fun ya
      Fuyu chikashi

—MURŌ SAISEI

固
く
な
る
目
白
の
糞
や
冬
近
し

室生　犀生

Note: The *mejiro* (white-eye) is a small Japanese bird with rings of feathers around the eyes.

Murō Saisei (1889–1962) was an illegitimate child who left school in the seventh grade. A haiku master in his hometown of Kanazawa introduced him to literature. Saisei wrote poems and novels about love, solitude, and loneliness.

The Oku-Shirane Range
Brightens with the snow
Of the world beyond.

Oku-Shirane
Kano yo no yuki o
Kagayakasu

—MAEDA FURA

Note: Oku-Shirane is the general name for a group of three mountains in western Yamanashi prefecture.

Maeda Fura (1884–1954) left Waseda University and became a journalist. After retiring from the newspaper, he founded the haiku magazine *Kobushi* (cucumber tree). He lived in a mountainous area and composed brilliant haiku about the hills and mountains.

In vain a winter bee
Went on tottering
For a place to die.

Fuyu-bachi no
Shini-dokoro naku
Aruki keri

—MURAKAMI KIJŌ

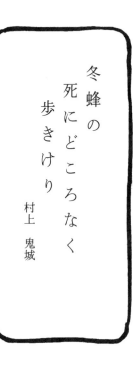

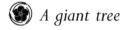 *A giant tree*
   Rises up into the clouds
      On the withered field.

Taiboku no
   Kumo ni sobiyuru
      Kare-no kana

—MASAOKA SHIKI

大木の
雲にそびゆる
枯野哉

正岡 子規

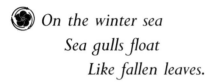 *On the winter sea*
 Sea gulls float
 Like fallen leaves.

Fuyu umi ya

Rakka no gotoku

Kamome uku

—NAKAMURA KUSATAO

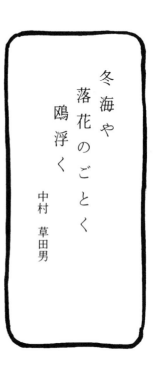

Nakamura Kusatao (1901–83) was born in China, where his father was in the diplomatic corps. In 1933 Kusatao became a contributor to the magazine *Hototogisu*, founded by Masaoka Shiki. He later became disillusioned with the mere description of nature and in 1946 left *Hototogisu* to establish *Banryoku* (greenery all around).

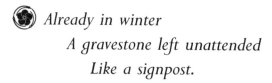 *Already in winter*
A gravestone left unattended
Like a signpost.

Fuyu sude-ni
Rohyō ni magau
Haka ikki

—NAKAMURA KUSATAO

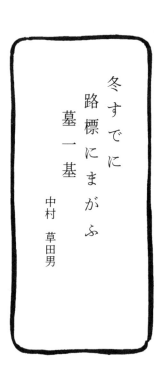

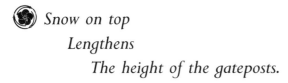 *Snow on top*
   Lengthens
      The height of the gateposts.

Monchū no
   Se-take o nobasu
      Kaburi yuki

—MIURA YUZURU

門柱の
背丈を伸ばす
冠雪

三浦 謙

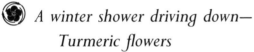 *A winter shower driving down—*
   Turmeric flowers
   In full bloom.

Shigure hase
   Ukon no hana no
      Sakari naru

—ŌNO RINKA

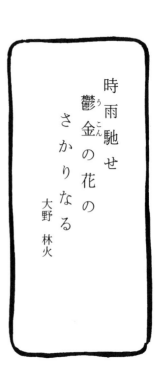

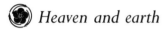 *Heaven and earth*
　　Convulsing in the same breath
　　Let fall a tremendous snow.

Ame-tsuchi no
　Iki aite hageshi
　　Yuki furasu

　　　　　—NOZAWA SETSUKO

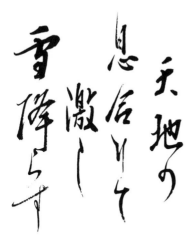

 *Winter roses*
Are a dazzling sight
To the eyes of an invalid.

Yamu hitomi niwa
Mabushiki mono ka
Fuyu sōbi

—KATŌ SHŪSON

Born in Tokyo in 1905, Katō Shūson at first contributed poetry to *Ashibi* or *Asebi* (Japanese andromeda), founded by Mizuhara Shūōshi. Later he turned from the lyrical style of *Ashibi* to an introspective style of haiku. During the 1930s he was called a poet of the "human quest school" of haiku. In 1940 he founded the haiku magazine *Kanrai* (thunder in midwinter).

While cutting the cake on Christmas Eve
　　My rogue self
　　　　Shrinking away.

Seika kiru
　　Toki ni burai o
　　　　Tōkushite

　　　　—KADOKAWA HARUKI

Note: The poem was written on Christmas Eve, the birthday of the poet's child.

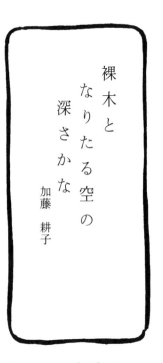

Through the branches of a tree
  Utterly leafless
    The sky deepens.

Hadaka-gi to
  Naritaru sora no
    Fukasa kana

—KATŌ KŌKO

Born in Kyoto in 1931, Katō Kōko started to write poetry under the influence of her grandfather. In 1978 she became a contributor to the
magazine *Obi* (sash), a branch group of the magazine *Ashibi*. In 1986 she
initiated the magazine *Kō* (cultivation), which publishes haiku in both
Japanese and English. She is now playing an active role in popularizing
haiku outside Japan.

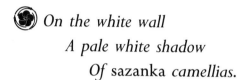 *On the white wall*
A pale white shadow
Of sazanka *camellias.*

Sazanka ya
Shira-kabe awaki
Shiroki kage

—ISHIZAKI RYOKUFŪ

Note: Sazanka is a tree of the tea family cultivated for hedges. Toward
the end of autumn five-petaled flowers of red, pink, or white bloom.

Born in Toyama prefecture in 1935, Ishizaki Ryokufū is a businessman
working for Komatsu, Ltd., a construction-equipment manufacturer in
Tokyo. In 1986 he became a contributor to the haiku magazine *Kō* and
is now one of its most influential members.

NEW YEAR'S

新年

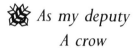 *As my deputy*
  A crow
    Is bathing in New Year's water.

Myōdai ni
  Waka-mizu abiru
    Karasu kana

—KOBAYASHI ISSA

名代に
わか水浴る
烏かな

小林　一茶

Note: The word *waka-mizu* means the first water drawn on New Year's morning.

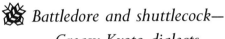 *Battledore and shuttlecock—*
Greasy Kyoto dialects
Pop out.

Yari-hago ya
   Abura no yō na
     Kyō-kotoba

       —TAKAHAMA KYOSHI

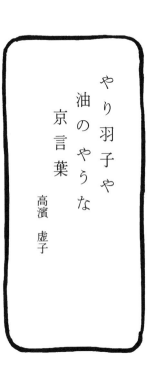

Note: Battledore and shuttlecock, an early form of badminton, is commonly played on New Year's Day.

On New Year's Day
The mountains brighten
In the snow.

Ganjitsu ya
   Yama ake kakaru
      Yuki no naka

—MURŌ SAISEI

元日や
山明けかかる
雪の中

室生 犀生

 *On New Year's Day*
  Mt. Fuji presents a brilliant figure
    Above the tea hills.

Hatsu-Fuji ya
  Cha-zan no ue ni
    Kakure nashi

—TOMIYASU FŪSEI

初
富
士
や
茶
山
の
上
に
か
く
れ
な
し
　富安　風生

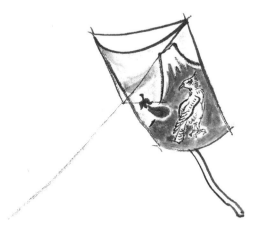

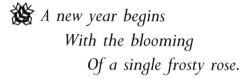 *A new year begins*
With the blooming
Of a single frosty rose.

Ichi-rin no
Shimo no bara yori
Toshi akuru

—MIZUHARA SHŪŌSHI

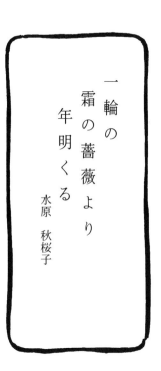

一輪の
霜の薔薇より
年明くる

水原　秋桜子

A watching crane
  Whoops far and wide
    As the dawn approaches.

Mi-hari tsuru
  Yo-ake to tomo ni
    Naki wataru

—MIURA YUZURU

見張鶴
夜明けとともに
啼きわたる
三浦 謙

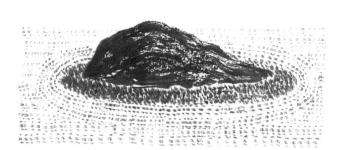